EXTRACTS FROM
ADAM'S
DIARY

AND FROM
EVE'S
DIARY

TRANSLATED FROM THE
ORIGINAL MANUSCRIPTS BY

APPLEWOOD BOOKS
BEDFORD, MASSACHUSETTS

Extracts from Adam's Diary
was originally published in 1897.
"Memoirs of the First Man" was translated from the
original manuscript and written down by Mark Twain.

———

Extracts from Eve's Diary
was originally published in 1905.
"Memoirs of the First Woman" was translated from the
original manuscript and written down by Mark Twain.

Thank you for purchasing an Applewood Book.
Applewood reprints America's lively classics—books from the
past that are still of interest to modern readers.
For a free copy of our current catalog, write to:

Applewood Books
P.O. Box 365
Bedford, MA 01730
www.awb.com

ISBN 978-1-55709-498-8

Library of Congress Catalog Card Number: 00-105702

MANUFACTURED IN THE U.S.A.

Extracts
From Adam's Diary

Translated from the original MS.

[NOTE. — *I translated a portion of this diary some years ago, and a friend of mine printed a few copies in an incomplete form, but the public never got them. Since then I have deciphered some more of Adam's hieroglyphics, and think he has now become sufficiently important as a public character to justify this publication.*—M. T.]

Extracts
From Adam's Diary

Translated from the original MS.

Monday

This new creature with the long hair is a good deal in the way. It is always hanging around and following me about. I don't like this; I am not used to company. I wish it would stay with the other animals. . . . Cloudy to-day, wind in the east; think we shall have rain. . . . *We?* Where did I get that word? . . . I remember now—the new creature uses it.

Tuesday

Been examining the great waterfall. It is the finest thing on the estate, I think. The new creature calls it Niagara Falls—why, I am sure I do not know. Says it *looks* like Niagara Falls. That is not a reason; it is mere waywardness and imbecility. I get no chance to name anything myself. The new creature names everything that comes along, before I can get in a protest. And always that same pretext is offered—it *looks* like the thing. There is the dodo, for instance. Says the moment one looks at it one sees at a glance that it "looks like a dodo." It will have to keep that name, no doubt. It wearies me to fret about it, and it does no good, anyway. Dodo! It looks no more like a dodo than I do.

4

Extracts from Adam's Diary

Wednesday

Built me a shelter against the rain, but could not have it to myself in peace. The new creature intruded. When I tried to put it out it shed water out of the holes it looks with, and wiped it away with the back of its paws, and made a noise such as some of the other animals make when they are in distress. I wish it would not talk; it is always talking. That sounds like a cheap fling at the poor creature, a slur; but I do not mean it so. I have never heard the human voice before, and any new and strange sound intruding itself here upon the solemn hush of these dreaming solitudes offends my ear and seems a false note. And this new sound is so close to me; it is right at my shoulder, right at my ear, first on one side and

Extracts from Adam's Diary

Wednesday

then on the other, and I am used only
to sounds that are more or less dis-
tant from me.

Extracts from Adam's Diary

Friday

The naming goes recklessly on, in spite of anything I can do. I had a very good name for the estate, and it was musical and pretty—GARDEN-OF-EDEN. Privately, I continue to call it that, but not any longer publicly. The new creature says it is all woods and rocks and scenery, and therefore has no resemblance to a garden. Says it *looks* like a park, and does not look like anything *but* a park. Consequently, without consulting me, it has been new-named —NIAGARA FALLS PARK. This is sufficiently high-handed, it seems to me. And already there is a sign up:

> KEEP OFF
> THE GRASS

My life is not as happy as it was.

Extracts from Adam's Diary

Saturday

The new creature eats too much
fruit. We are going to run short,
most likely. "We" again—that is
its word; mine too, now, from hearing
it so much. Good deal of fog this
morning. I do not go out in the fog
myself. The new creature does. It
goes out in all weathers, and stumps
right in with its muddy feet. And
talks. It used to be so pleasant and
quiet here.

Extracts from Adam's Diary

Sunday

Pulled through. This day is getting to be more and more trying. It was selected and set apart last November as a day of rest. I already had six of them per week, before. This morning found the new creature trying to clod apples out of that forbidden tree.

Monday

The new creature says its name is Eve. That is all right, I have no objections. Says it is to call it by when I want it to come. I said it was superfluous, then. The word evidently raised me in its respect; and indeed it is a large, good word, and will bear repetition. It says it is not an It, it is a She. This is probably doubtful; yet it is all one to me; what she is were nothing to me if she would but go by herself and not talk.

Extracts from Adam's Diary

Tuesday

She has littered the whole estate with execrable names and offensive signs:

☞ THIS WAY TO THE WHIRLPOOL.

☞ THIS WAY TO GOAT ISLAND.

☞ CAVE OF THE WINDS THIS WAY.

She says this park would make a tidy summer resort, if there was any custom for it. Summer resort—another invention of hers—just words, without any meaning. What is a summer resort? But it is best not to ask her, she has such a rage for explaining.

11

Friday

She has taken to beseeching me to stop going over the Falls. What harm does it do? Says it makes her shudder. I wonder why. I have always done it — always liked the plunge, and the excitement, and the coolness. I supposed it was what the Falls were for. They have no other use that I can see, and they must have been made for something. She says they were only made for scenery— like the rhinoceros and the mastodon.

I went over the Falls in a barrel— not satisfactory to her. Went over in a tub—still not satisfactory. Swam the Whirlpool and the Rapids in a fig-leaf suit. It got much damaged. Hence, tedious complaints about my extravagance. I am too much hampered here. What I need is change of scene.

12

Saturday

I escaped last Tuesday night, and travelled two days, and built me another shelter, in a secluded place, and obliterated my tracks as well as I could, but she hunted me out by means of a beast which she has tamed and calls a wolf, and came making that pitiful noise again, and shedding that water out of the places she looks with. I was obliged to return with her, but will presently emigrate again, when occasion offers. She engages herself in many foolish things: among others, trying to study out why the animals called lions and tigers live on grass and flowers, when, as she says, the sort of teeth they wear would indicate that they were intended to eat each other. This is foolish, because to do that would be

13

Saturday

to kill each other, and that would introduce what, as I understand it, is called "death"; and death, as I have been told, has not yet entered the Park. Which is a pity, on some accounts.

14

Extracts from Adam's Diary

Sunday

    Pulled through.

Extracts from Adam's Diary

Monday

I believe I see what the week is for: it is to give time to rest up from the weariness of Sunday. It seems a good idea. . . . She has been climbing that tree again. Clodded her out of it. She said nobody was looking. Seems to consider that a sufficient justification for chancing any dangerous thing. Told her that. The word justification moved her admiration— and envy too, I thought. It is a good word.

Thursday

She told me she was made out of a rib taken from my body. This is at least doubtful, if not more than that. I have not missed any rib. . . . She is in much trouble about the buzzard; says grass does not agree with it; is afraid she can't raise it; thinks it was intended to live on decayed flesh. The buzzard must get along the best it can with what is provided. We cannot overturn the whole scheme to accommodate the buzzard.

Saturday

She fell in the pond yesterday, when she was looking at herself in it, which she is always doing. She nearly strangled, and said it was most uncomfortable. This made her sorry for the creatures which live in there, which she calls fish, for she continues to fasten names on to things that don't need them and don't come when they are called by them, which is a matter of no consequence to her, as she is such a numskull anyway; so she got a lot of them out and brought them in last night and put them in my bed to keep warm, but I have noticed them now and then all day, and I don't see that they are any happier there than they were before, only quieter. When night comes I shall throw them out-doors. I will not

Extracts from Adam's Diary

Saturday

sleep with them again, for I find them clammy and unpleasant to lie among when a person hasn't anything on.

Extracts from Adam's Diary

Sunday
　　Pulled through.

Extracts from Adam's Diary

Tuesday

She has taken up with a snake now. The other animals are glad, for she was always experimenting with them and bothering them; and I am glad, because the snake talks, and this enables me to get a rest.

Extracts from Adam's Diary

Friday

She says the snake advises her to try the fruit of that tree, and says the result will be a great and fine and noble education. I told her there would be another result, too — it would introduce death into the world. That was a mistake—it had been better to keep the remark to myself; it only gave her an idea—she could save the sick buzzard, and furnish fresh meat to the despondent lions and tigers. I advised her to keep away from the tree. She said she wouldn't. I foresee trouble. Will emigrate.

22

Wednesday

I have had a variegated time. I escaped that night, and rode a horse all night as fast as he could go, hoping to get clear out of the Park and hide in some other country before the trouble should begin; but it was not to be. About an hour after sunup, as I was riding through a flowery plain where thousands of animals were grazing, slumbering, or playing with each other, according to their wont, all of a sudden they broke into a tempest of frightful noises, and in one moment the plain was in a frantic commotion and every beast was destroying its neighbor. I knew what it meant—Eve had eaten that fruit, and death was come into the world. . . . The tigers ate my horse, paying no attention when I ordered them to

23

Wednesday

desist, and they would even have
eaten me if I had stayed—which I
didn't, but went away in much haste.
. . . I found this place, outside the
Park, and was fairly comfortable for
a few days, but she has found me
out. Found me out, and has named
the place Tonawanda—says it *looks*
like that. In fact, I was not sorry
she came, for there are but meagre
pickings here, and she brought some
of those apples. I was obliged to
eat them, I was so hungry. It was
against my principles, but I find that
principles have no real force except
when one is well fed. . . . She came
curtained in boughs and bunches of
leaves, and when I asked her what
she meant by such nonsense, and
snatched them away and threw them

24

Extracts from Adam's Diary

Wednesday

down, she tittered and blushed. I
had never seen a person titter and
blush before, and to me it seemed un-
becoming and idiotic. She said I
would soon know how it was myself.
This was correct. Hungry as I was, I
laid down the apple half eaten—certainly the best one I ever saw, con-
sidering the lateness of the season—
and arrayed myself in the discarded
boughs and branches, and then spoke
to her with some severity and ordered
her to go and get some more and not
make such a spectacle of herself.
She did it, and after this we crept
down to where the wild-beast battle
had been, and collected some skins,
and I made her patch together a
couple of suits proper for public oc-
casions. They are uncomfortable, it

Extracts from Adam's Diary

Wednesday

is true, but stylish, and that is the main point about clothes. . . . I find she is a good deal of a companion. I see I should be lonesome and depressed without her, now that I have lost my property. Another thing, she says it is ordered that we work for our living hereafter. She will be useful. I will superintend.

Extracts from Adam's Diary

Ten Days Later

She accuses *me* of being the cause of our disaster! She says, with apparent sincerity and truth, that the Serpent assured her that the forbidden fruit was not apples, it was chestnuts. I said I was innocent, then, for I had not eaten any chestnuts. She said the Serpent informed her that "chestnut" was a figurative term meaning an aged and mouldy joke. I turned pale at that, for I have made many jokes to pass the weary time, and some of them could have been of that sort, though I had honestly supposed that they were new when I made them. She asked me if I had made one just at the time of the catastrophe. I was obliged to admit that I had made one to myself, though not aloud. It was this.

Ten Days Later

I was thinking about the Falls, and I said to myself, "How wonderful it is to see that vast body of water tumble down there!" Then in an instant a bright thought flashed into my head, and I let it fly, saying, "It would be a deal more wonderful to see it tumble *up* there!"—and I was just about to kill myself with laughing at it when all nature broke loose in war and death, and I had to flee for my life. "There," she said, with triumph, "that is just it; the Serpent mentioned that very jest, and called it the First Chestnut, and said it was coeval with the creation." Alas, I am indeed to blame. Would that I were not witty; oh, would that I had never had that radiant thought!

Next Year

We have named it Cain. She
caught it while I was up country
trapping on the North Shore of the
Erie; caught it in the timber a couple
of miles from our dug - out — or it
might have been four, she isn't certain which. It resembles us in some
ways, and may be a relation. That
is what she thinks, but this is an error,
in my judgment. The difference in
size warrants the conclusion that it
is a different and new kind of animal
—a fish, perhaps, though when I put
it in the water to see, it sank, and she
plunged in and snatched it out before
there was opportunity for the experiment to determine the matter.
I still think it is a fish, but she is indifferent about what it is, and will
not let me have it to try. I do not

29

Next Year

understand this. The coming of the
creature seems to have changed her
whole nature and made her unrea-
sonable about experiments. She
thinks more of it than she does of any
of the other animals, but is not able
to explain why. Her mind is dis-
ordered—everything shows it. Sometimes she carries the fish in her arms
half the night when it complains and
wants to get to the water. At such
times the water comes out of the
places in her face that she looks out
of, and she pats the fish on the back
and makes soft sounds with her
mouth to soothe it, and betrays sorrow and solicitude in a hundred ways.
I have never seen her do like this
with any other fish, and it troubles
me greatly. She used to carry the

30

Next Year

young tigers around so, and play
with them, before we lost our property; but it was only play; she never
took on about them like this when
their dinner disagreed with them.

Sunday

She doesn't work Sundays, but lies around all tired out, and likes to have the fish wallow over her; and she makes fool noises to amuse it, and pretends to chew its paws, and that makes it laugh. I have not seen a fish before that could laugh. This makes me doubt. . . . I have come to like Sunday myself. Superintending all the week tires a body so. There ought to be more Sundays. In the old days they were tough, but now they come handy.

Extracts from Adam's Diary

Wednesday

It isn't a fish. I cannot quite make out what it is. It makes curious, devilish noises when not satisfied, and says "goo-goo" when it is. It is not one of us, for it doesn't walk; it is not a bird, for it doesn't fly; it is not a frog, for it doesn't hop; it is not a snake, for it doesn't crawl; I feel sure it is not a fish, though I cannot get a chance to find out whether it can swim or not. It merely lies around, and mostly on its back, with its feet up. I have not seen any other animal do that before. I said I believed it was an enigma, but she only admired the word without understanding it. In my judgment it is either an enigma or some kind of a bug. If it dies, I will take it apart and see what its arrangements are. I never had a thing perplex me so.

33

Extracts from Adam's Diary

Three Months Later

The perplexity augments instead
of diminishing. I sleep but little.
It has ceased from lying around, and
goes about on its four legs now. Yet
it differs from the other four-legged
animals in that its front legs are
unusually short, consequently this
causes the main part of its person to
stick up uncomfortably high in the
air, and this is not attractive. It is
built much as we are, but its method
of travelling shows that it is not of
our breed. The short front legs and
long hind ones indicate that it is of
the kangaroo family, but it is a
marked variation of the species, since
the true kangaroo hops, whereas this
one never does. Still, it is a curious
and interesting variety, and has not
been catalogued before. As I dis-

Three Months Later

covered it, I have felt justified in se-
curing the credit of the discovery by
attaching my name to it, and hence
have called it *Kangaroorum Adam-
iensis*. . . . It must have been a young
one when it came, for it has grown
exceedingly since. It must be five
times as big, now, as it was then,
and when discontented is able to
make from twenty-two to thirty-
eight times the noise it made at first.
Coercion does not modify this, but has
the contrary effect. For this reason
I discontinued the system. She rec-
onciles it by persuasion, and by giv-
ing it things which she had previously
told it she wouldn't give it. As already observed, I was not at home
when it first came, and she told me
she found it in the woods. It seems

35

Extracts from Adam's Diary

Three Months Later

odd that it should be the only one,
yet it must be so, for I have worn
myself out these many weeks trying
to find another one to add to my
collection, and for this one to play
with; for surely then it would be
quieter, and we could tame it more
easily. But I find none, nor any
vestige of any; and strangest of all,
no tracks. It has to live on the
ground, it cannot help itself; therefore, how does it get about without
leaving a track? I have set a dozen
traps, but they do no good. I catch
all small animals except that one;
animals that merely go into the trap
out of curiosity, I think, to see what
the milk is there for. They never
drink it.

Three Months Later

The kangaroo still continues to grow, which is very strange and perplexing. I never knew one to be so long getting its growth. It has fur on its head now; not like kangaroo fur, but exactly like our hair, except that it is much finer and softer, and instead of being black is red. I am like to lose my mind over the capricious and harassing developments of this unclassifiable zoological freak. If I could catch another one—but that is hopeless; it is a new variety, and the only sample; this is plain. But I caught a true kangaroo and brought it in, thinking that this one, being lonesome, would rather have that for company than have no kin at all, or any animal it could feel a nearness to or get sympathy from in

Three Months Later

its forlorn condition here among strangers who do not know its ways or habits, or what to do to make it feel that it is among friends; but it was a mistake—it went into such fits at the sight of the kangaroo that I was convinced it had never seen one before. I pity the poor noisy little animal, but there is nothing I can do to make it happy. If I could tame it—but that is out of the question; the more I try, the worse I seem to make it. It grieves me to the heart to see it in its little storms of sorrow and passion. I wanted to let it go, but she wouldn't hear of it. That seemed cruel and not like her; and yet she may be right. It might be lonelier than ever; for since I cannot find another one, how could *it?*

38

Five Months Later

It is not a kangaroo. No, for it supports itself by holding to her finger, and thus goes a few steps on its hind legs, and then falls down. It is probably some kind of a bear; and yet it has no tail—as yet—and no fur, except on its head. It still keeps on growing—that is a curious circumstance, for bears get their growth earlier than this. Bears are dangerous—since our catastrophe—and I shall not be satisfied to have this one prowling about the place much longer without a muzzle on. I have offered to get her a kangaroo if she would let this one go, but it did no good—she is determined to run us into all sorts of foolish risks, I think. She was not like this before she lost her mind.

A Fortnight Later

I examined its mouth. There is no danger yet; it has only one tooth. It has no tail yet. It makes more noise now than it ever did before — and mainly at night. I have moved out. But I shall go over, mornings, to breakfast, and to see if it has more teeth. If it gets a mouthful of teeth, it will be time for it to go, tail or no tail, for a bear does not need a tail in order to be dangerous.

40

Four Months Later

I have been off hunting and fishing a month, up in the region that she calls Buffalo; I don't know why, unless it is because there are not any buffaloes there. Meantime the bear has learned to paddle around all by itself on its hind legs, and says "poppa" and "momma." It is certainly a new species. This resemblance to words may be purely accidental, of course, and may have no purpose or meaning; but even in that case it is still extraordinary, and is a thing which no other bear can do. This imitation of speech, taken together with general absence of fur and entire absence of tail, sufficiently indicates that this is a new kind of bear. The further study of it will be exceedingly interesting. Meantime I will go off

41

Extracts from Adam's Diary

Four Months Later

on a far expedition among the forests
of the North and make an exhaustive
search. There must certainly be another one somewhere, and this one
will be less dangerous when it has
company of its own species. I will
go straightway; but I will muzzle this
one first.

Three Months Later

It has been a weary, weary hunt, yet I have had no success. In the mean time, without stirring from the home estate, she has caught another one! I never saw such luck. I might have hunted these woods a hundred years, I never should have run across that thing.

Next Day

I have been comparing the new one with the old one, and it is perfectly plain that they are the same breed. I was going to stuff one of them for my collection, but she is prejudiced against it for some reason or other; so I have relinquished the idea, though I think it is a mistake. It would be an irreparable loss to science if they should get away. The old one is tamer than it was, and can laugh and talk like the parrot, having learned this, no doubt, from being with the parrot so much, and having the imitative faculty in a highly developed degree. I shall be astonished if it turns out to be a new kind of parrot; and yet I ought not to be astonished, for it has already been everything else it could think of, since those

44

Next Day

first days when it was a fish. The
new one is as ugly now as the old one
was at first; has the same sulphur-
and-raw-meat complexion and the
same singular head without any fur
on it. She calls it Abel.

Extracts from Adam's Diary

Ten Years Later

They are boys; we found it out long ago. It was their coming in that small, immature shape that puzzled us; we were not used to it. There are some girls now. Abel is a good boy, but if Cain had stayed a bear it would have improved him. After all these years, I see that I was mistaken about Eve in the beginning; it is better to live outside the Garden with her than inside it without her. At first I thought she talked too much; but now I should be sorry to have that voice fall silent and pass out of my life. Blessed be the chestnut that brought us near together and taught me to know the goodness of her heart and the sweetness of her spirit!

THE END

46

Eve's Diary

Translated from the Original

Eve's Diary

Translated from the Original

Saturday

I am almost a whole day old, now. I arrived yesterday. That is as it seems to me. And it must be so, for if there was a day-before-yesterday I was not there when it happened, or I should remember it. It could be, of course, that it did happen, and that I was not noticing. Very well; I will be very watchful, now, and if any day-before-yesterdays happen I will make a note of it. It will be best to start right and not let the record get confused, for some instinct tells me that these details are going to be important to the historian some day.

Saturday

For I feel like an experiment, I feel exactly like an experiment; it would be impossible for a person to feel more like an experiment than I do, and so I am coming to feel convinced that that is what I *am* — an experiment; just an experiment, and nothing more.

Then if I am an experiment, am I the whole of it? No, I think not; I think the rest of it is part of it. I am the main part of it, but I think the rest of it has its share in the matter. Is my position assured, or do I have to watch it and take care of it? The latter, perhaps. Some instinct tells me that eternal vigilance is the price of supremacy. [That is a good phrase, I think, for one so young.]

Everything looks better to-day than it did yesterday. In the rush

50

Saturday

of finishing up yesterday, the mountains were left in a ragged condition, and some of the plains were so cluttered with rubbish and remnants that the aspects were quite distressing. Noble and beautiful works of art should not be subjected to haste; and this majestic new world is indeed a most noble and beautiful work. And certainly marvellously near to being perfect, notwithstanding the shortness of the time. There are too many stars in some places and not enough in others, but that can be remedied presently, no doubt. The moon got loose last night, and slid down and fell out of the scheme—a very great loss; it breaks my heart to think of it. There isn't another thing among the ornaments and dec-

Saturday

orations that is comparable to it for beauty and finish. It should have been fastened better. If we can only get it back again—

But of course there is no telling where it went to. And besides, whoever gets it will hide it; I know it because I would do it myself. I believe I can be honest in all other matters, but I already begin to realize that the core and centre of my nature is love of the beautiful, a passion for the beautiful, and that it would not be safe to trust me with a moon that belonged to another person and that person didn't know I had it. I could give up a moon that I found in the daytime, because I should be afraid some one was looking; but if I found it in the dark, I am sure I should find

Saturday

some kind of an excuse for not saying anything about it. For I do love moons, they are so pretty and so romantic. I wish we had five or six; I would never go to bed; I should never get tired lying on the moss-bank and looking up at them.

Stars are good, too. I wish I could get some to put in my hair. But I suppose I never can. You would be surprised to find how far off they are, for they do not look it. When they first showed, last night, I tried to knock some down with a pole, but it didn't reach, which astonished me; then I tried clods till I was all tired out, but I never got one. It was because I am left-handed and cannot throw good. Even when I aimed at the one I wasn't after I couldn't hit

Saturday

the other one, though I did make
some close shots, for I saw the black
blot of the clod sail right into the
midst of the golden clusters forty or
fifty times, just barely missing them,
and if I could have held out a little
longer maybe I could have got one.

So I cried a little, which was natural, I suppose, for one of my age,
and after I was rested I got a basket
and started for a place on the ex-
treme rim of the circle, where the
stars were close to the ground and I
could get them with my hands, which
would be better, anyway, because I
could gather them tenderly then, and
not break them. But it was farther
than I thought, and at last I had to
give it up; I was so tired I couldn't
drag my feet another step; and be-

54

Saturday

sides, they were sore and hurt me
very much.

I couldn't get back home; it was
too far, and turning cold; but I found
some tigers, and nestled in among
them and was most adorably comfortable, and their breath was sweet
and pleasant, because they live on
strawberries. I had never seen a
tiger before, but I knew them in a
minute by the stripes. If I could
have one of those skins, it would
make a lovely gown.

To-day I am getting better ideas
about distances. I was so eager to
get hold of every pretty thing that I
giddily grabbed for it, sometimes
when it was too far off, and sometimes when it was but six inches
away but seemed a foot—alas, with

55

Saturday

thorns between! I learned a lesson; also I made an axiom, all out of my own head — my very first one: *The scratched Experiment shuns the thorn.* I think it is a very good one for one so young.

I followed the other Experiment around, yesterday afternoon, at a distance, to see what it might be for, if I could. But I was not able to make out. I think it is a man. I had never seen a man, but it looked like one, and I feel sure that that is what it is. I realize that I feel more curiosity about it than about any of the other reptiles. If it is a reptile, and I suppose it is; for it has frowsy hair and blue eyes, and looks like a reptile. It has no hips; it tapers like a carrot; when it stands, it spreads

Saturday

itself apart like a derrick; so I think it is a reptile, though it may be architecture.

I was afraid of it at first, and started to run every time it turned around, for I thought it was going to chase me; but by-and-by I found it was only trying to get away, so after that I was not timid any more, but tracked it along, several hours, about twenty yards behind, which made it nervous and unhappy. At last it was a good deal worried, and climbed a tree. I waited a good while, then gave it up and went home.

To-day the same thing over. I've got it up the tree again.

57

Sunday

It is up there yet. Resting, apparently. But that is a subterfuge: Sunday isn't the day of rest; Saturday is appointed for that. It looks to me like a creature that is more interested in resting than in anything else. It would tire me to rest so much. It tires me just to sit around and watch the tree. I do wonder what it is for; I never see it do anything.

They returned the moon last night, and I was *so* happy! I think it is very honest of them. It slid down and fell off again, but I was not distressed; there is no need to worry when one has that kind of neighbors; they will fetch it back. I wish I could do something to show my appreciation. I would like to *send*

58

Sunday

them some stars, for we have more
than we can use. I mean I, not we,
for I can see that the reptile cares
nothing for such things.

It has low tastes, and is not kind.
When I went there yesterday even-
ing in the gloaming it had crept down
and was trying to catch the little
speckled fishes that play in the pool,
and I had to clod it to make it go
up the tree again and let them alone.
I wonder if *that* is what it is for?
Hasn't it any heart? Hasn't it any
compassion for those little creatures?
Can it be that it was designed and
manufactured for such ungentle work?
It has the look of it. One of the
clods took it back of the ear, and it
used language. It gave me a thrill,
for it was the first time I had ever

Sunday

heard speech, except my own. I did not understand the words, but they seemed expressive.

When I found it could talk, I felt a new interest in it, for I love to talk; I talk all day, and in my sleep, too, and I am very interesting, but if I had another to talk to I could be twice as interesting, and would never stop, if desired.

If this reptile is a man, it isn't an *it*, is it? That wouldn't be grammatical, would it? I think it would be *he*. I think so. In that case one would parse it thus: nominative, *he;* dative, *him;* possessive, *his'n*. Well, I will consider it a man and call it he until it turns out to be something else. This will be handier than having so many uncertainties.

Next week Sunday

All the week I tagged around after him and tried to get acquainted. I had to do the talking, because he was shy, but I didn't mind it. He seemed pleased to have me around, and I used the sociable "we" a good deal, because it seemed to flatter him to be included.

Wednesday

We are getting along very well indeed, now, and getting better and better acquainted. He does not try to avoid me any more, which is a good sign, and shows that he likes to have me with him. That pleases me, and I study to be useful to him in every way I can, so as to increase his regard. During the last day or two I have taken all the work of naming things off his hands, and this has been a great relief to him, for he has no gift in that line, and is evidently very grateful. He can't think of a rational name to save him, but I do not let him see that I am aware of his defect. Whenever a new creature comes along, I name it before he has time to expose himself by an awkward silence. In this way I have

62

Wednesday

saved him many embarrassments. I have no defect like his. The minute I set eyes on an animal I know what it is. I don't have to reflect a moment; the right name comes out instantly, just as if it were an inspiration, as no doubt it is, for I am sure it wasn't in me half a minute before. I seem to know just by the shape of the creature and the way it acts what animal it is.

When the dodo came along he thought it was a wildcat—I saw it in his eye. But I saved him. And I was careful not to do it in a way that could hurt his pride. I just spoke up in a quite natural way of pleased surprise, and not as if I was dreaming of conveying information, and said, "Well, I do declare if there

Wednesday

isn't the dodo!" I explained—without seeming to be explaining—how I knew it for a dodo, and although I thought maybe he was a little piqued that I knew the creature when he didn't, it was quite evident that he admired me. That was very agreeable, and I thought of it more than once with gratification before I slept. How little a thing can make us happy when we feel that we have earned it.

Thursday

My first sorrow. Yesterday he avoided me and seemed to wish I would not talk to him. I could not believe it, and thought there was some mistake, for I loved to be with him, and loved to hear him talk, and so how could it be that he could feel unkind towards me when I had not done anything? But at last it seemed true, so I went away and sat lonely in the place where I first saw him the morning that we were made and I did not know what he was and was indifferent about him; but now it was a mournful place, and every little thing spoke of him, and my heart was very sore. I did not know why very clearly, for it was a new feeling; I had not experienced it before, and it was all a mys-

Thursday

tery, and I could not make it out.

But when night came I could not bear the lonesomeness, and went to the new shelter which he has built, to ask him what I had done that was wrong and how I could mend it and get back his kindness again; but he put me out in the rain, and it was my first sorrow.

Sunday

It is pleasant again, now, and I am happy; but those were heavy days; I do not think of them when I can help it.

I tried to get him some of those apples, but I cannot learn to throw straight. I failed, but I think the good intention pleased him. They are forbidden, and he says I shall come to harm; but so I come to harm through pleasing him, why shall I care for that harm?

Eve's Diary

Monday

This morning I told him my name, hoping it would interest him. But he did not care for it. It is strange. If he should tell me his name, I would care. I think it would be pleasanter in my ears than any other sound.

He talks very little. Perhaps it is because he is not bright, and is sensitive about it and wishes to conceal it. It is such a pity that he should feel so, for brightness is nothing; it is in the heart that the values lie. I wish I could make him understand that a loving good heart is riches, and riches enough, and that without it intellect is poverty.

Although he talks so little he has quite a considerable vocabulary. This morning he used a surprisingly good word. He evidently recognized, him-

Monday

self, that it was a good one, for he worked it in twice afterwards, casually. It was not good casual art, still it showed that he possesses a certain quality of perception. Without a doubt that seed can be made to grow, if cultivated.

Where did he get that word? I do not think I have ever used it.

No, he took no interest in my name. I tried to hide my disappointment, but I suppose I did not succeed. I went away and sat on the moss-bank with my feet in the water. It is where I go when I hunger for companionship, some one to look at, some one to talk to. It is not enough—that lovely white body painted there in the pool—but it is something, and something is better than utter loneliness.

Monday

It talks when I talk; it is sad when
I am sad; it comforts me with its
sympathy; it says, "Do not be down-
hearted, you poor friendless girl; I
will be your friend." It *is* a good
friend to me, and my only one; it is
my sister.

That first time that she forsook me!
ah, I shall never forget that—never,
never. My heart was lead in my
body! I said, "She was all I had,
and now she is gone!" In my de-
spair I said, "Break, my heart; I cannot bear my life any more!" and hid
my face in my hands, and there was
no solace for me. And when I took
them away, after a little, there she
was again, white and shining and
beautiful, and I sprang into her arms!

That was perfect happiness; I had

70

Monday

known happiness before, but it was
not like this, which was ecstasy. I
never doubted her afterwards. Sometimes she stayed away—maybe an
hour, maybe almost the whole day,
but I waited and did not doubt; I
said, "She is busy, or she is gone a
journey, but she will come." And it
was so: she always did. At night she
would not come if it was dark, for
she was a timid little thing; but if
there was a moon she would come.
I am not afraid of the dark, but she
is younger than I am; she was born
after I was. Many and many are the
visits I have paid her; she is my com-
fort and my refuge when my life is
hard—and it is mainly that.

Tuesday

All the morning I was at work improving the estate; and I purposely kept away from him in the hope that he would get lonely and come. But he did not.

At noon I stopped for the day and took my recreation by flitting all about with the bees and the butterflies and revelling in the flowers, those beautiful creatures that catch the smile of God out of the sky and preserve it! I gathered them, and made them into wreaths and garlands and clothed myself in them while I ate my luncheon—apples, of course; then I sat in the shade and wished and waited. But he did not come.

But no matter. Nothing would have come of it, for he does not care

72

Tuesday

for flowers. He calls them rubbish, and cannot tell one from another, and thinks it is superior to feel like that. He does not care for me, he does not care for flowers, he does not care for the painted sky at eventide—is there anything he does care for, except building shacks to coop himself up in from the good clean rain, and thumping the melons, and sampling the grapes, and fingering the fruit on the trees, to see how those properties are coming along?

I laid a dry stick on the ground and tried to bore a hole in it with another one, in order to carry out a scheme that I had, and soon I got an awful fright. A thin, transparent, bluish film rose out of the hole, and I dropped everything and ran! I thought it

73

Tuesday

was a spirit, and I *was* so frightened!
But I looked back, and it was not
coming; so I leaned against a rock
and rested and panted, and let my
limbs go on trembling until they got
steady again; then I crept warily
back, alert, watching, and ready to
fly if there was occasion; and when I
was come near, I parted the branches
of a rose-bush and peeped through
—wishing the man was about, I was
looking so cunning and pretty—but
the sprite was gone. I went there,
and there was a pinch of delicate pink
dust in the hole. I put my finger in,
to feel it, and said *ouch!* and took
it out again. It was a cruel pain. I
put my finger in my mouth; and by
standing first on one foot and then
the other, and grunting, I presently

Tuesday

eased my misery; then I was full of
interest, and began to examine.

I was curious to know what the
pink dust was. Suddenly the name
of it occurred to me, though I had
never heard of it before. It was *fire!*
I was as certain of it as a person could
be of anything in the world. So
without hesitation I named it that—
fire.

I had created something that didn't
exist before; I had added a new thing
to the world's uncountable properties;
I realized this, and was proud of my
achievement, and was going to run
and find him and tell him about it,
thinking to raise myself in his esteem
—but I reflected, and did not do it.
No—he would not care for it. He
would ask what it was good for, and

Tuesday

what could I answer? For if it was not *good* for something, but only beautiful, merely beautiful—

So I sighed, and did not go. For it wasn't good for anything; it could not build a shack, it could not improve melons, it could not hurry a fruit crop; it was useless, it was a foolishness and a vanity; he would despise it and say cutting words. But to me it was not despicable; I said, "Oh, you fire, I love you, you dainty pink creature, for you are *beautiful*—and that is enough!" and was going to gather it to my breast. But refrained. Then I made another maxim out of my own head, though it was so nearly like the first one that I was afraid it was only a plagiarism: "*The burnt Experiment shuns the fire.*"

76

Tuesday

I wrought again; and when I had
made a good deal of fire-dust I emp-
tied it into a handful of dry brown
grass, intending to carry it home and
keep it always and play with it; but
the wind struck it and it sprayed up
and spat out at me fiercely, and I
dropped it and ran. When I looked
back the blue spirit was towering up
and stretching and rolling away like
a cloud, and instantly I thought of
the name of it—*smoke!*—though, upon
my word, I had never heard of smoke
before.

Soon, brilliant yellow-and-red flares
shot up through the smoke, and I
named them in an instant—*flames!*—
and I was right, too, though these
were the very first flames that had
ever been in the world. They climb-

Tuesday

ed the trees, they flashed splendidly
in and out of the vast and increasing
volume of tumbling smoke, and I had
to clap my hands and laugh and
dance in my rapture, it was so new
and strange and so wonderful and so
beautiful!

He came running, and stopped and
gazed, and said not a word for many
minutes. Then he asked what it was.
Ah, it was too bad that he should ask
such a direct question. I had to answer it, of course, and I did. I said
it was fire. If it annoyed him that
I should know and he must ask, that
was not my fault; I had no desire to
annoy him. After a pause he asked:

"How did it come?"

Another direct question, and it also
had to have a direct answer.

78

Tuesday

"I made it."

The fire was travelling farther and farther off. He went to the edge of the burned place and stood looking down, and said:

"What are these?"

"Fire-coals."

He picked up one to examine it, but changed his mind and put it down again. Then he went away. *Nothing* interests him.

But I was interested. There were ashes, gray and soft and delicate and pretty—I knew what they were at once. And the embers; I knew the embers, too. I found my apples, and raked them out, and was glad; for I am very young and my appetite is active. But I was disappointed; they were all burst open and spoiled.

79

Tuesday

Spoiled apparently; but it was not
so; they were better than raw ones.
Fire is beautiful; some day it will be
useful, I think.

Friday

I saw him again, for a moment, last Monday at nightfall, but only for a moment. I was hoping he would praise me for trying to improve the estate, for I had meant well and had worked hard. But he was not pleased, and turned away and left me. He was also displeased on another account: I tried once more to persuade him to stop going over the Falls. That was because the fire had revealed to me a new passion—quite new, and distinctly different from love, grief, and those others which I had already discovered—*fear*. And it is horrible!—I wish I had never discovered it; it gives me dark moments, it spoils my happiness, it makes me shiver and tremble and shudder. But I could not persuade

81

Eve's Diary

Friday

him, for he has not discovered fear yet, and so he could not understand me.

Extract from Adam's Diary

Perhaps I ought to remember that she is very young, a mere girl, and make allowances. She is all interest, eagerness, vivacity, the world is to her a charm, a wonder, a mystery, a joy; she can't speak for delight when she finds a new flower, she must pet it and caress it and smell it and talk to it, and pour out endearing names upon it. And she is color-mad: brown rocks, yellow sand, gray moss, green foliage, blue sky; the pearl of the dawn, the purple shadows on the mountains, the golden islands floating in crimson seas at sunset, the pallid moon sailing through the shredded cloud-rack, the

Friday

star-jewels glittering in the wastes of space—none of them is of any practical value, so far as I can see, but because they have color and majesty, that is enough for her, and she loses her mind over them. If she could quiet down and keep still a couple of minutes at a time, it would be a reposeful spectacle. In that case I think I could enjoy looking at her; indeed I am sure I could, for I am coming to realize that she is a quite remarkably comely creature — lithe, slender, trim, rounded, shapely, nimble, graceful; and once when she was standing marble-white and sun-drenched on a bowlder, with her young head tilted back and her hand shading her eyes, watching the flight of a bird in the sky, I recognized that she was beautiful.

Monday noon.—If there is any-

Friday

thing on the planet that she is not
interested in it is not in my list.
There are animals that I am indifferent to, but it is not so with her. She
has no discrimination, she takes to
all of them, she thinks they are all
treasures, every new one is welcome.

When the mighty brontosaurus came
striding into camp, she regarded it as
an acquisition, I considered it a ca-
lamity; that is a good sample of the
lack of harmony that prevails in our
views of things. She wanted to do-
mesticate it, I wanted to make it a
present of the homestead and move out.
She believed it could be tamed by kind
treatment and would be a good pet; I
said a pet twenty-one feet high and
eighty-four feet long would be no
proper thing to have about the place,
because, even with the best intentions
and without meaning any harm, it

84

Friday

could sit down on the house and mash it, for any one could see by the look of its eye that it was absent-minded.

Still, her heart was set upon having that monster, and she couldn't give it up. She thought we could start a dairy with it, and wanted me to help her milk it; but I wouldn't; it was too risky. The sex wasn't right, and we hadn't any ladder anyway. Then she wanted to ride it, and look at the scenery. Thirty or forty feet of its tail was lying on the ground, like a fallen tree, and she thought she could climb it, but she was mistaken; when she got to the steep place it was too slick and down she came, and would have hurt herself but for me.

Was she satisfied now? No. Nothing ever satisfies her but demonstration; untested theories are not in her line, and she won't have them. It is the right spirit, I concede it; it attracts

85

Friday

me; I feel the influence of it; if I were with her more I think I should take it up myself. Well, she had one theory remaining about this colossus: she thought that if we could tame him and make him friendly we could stand him in the river and use him for a bridge. It turned out that he was already plenty tame enough—at least as far as she was concerned—so she tried her theory, but it failed; every time she got him properly placed in the river and went ashore to cross over on him, he came out and followed her around like a pet mountain. Like the other animals. They all do that.

Tuesday — Wednesday — Thursday —and to-day: all without seeing him. It is a long time to be alone; still, it is better to be alone than unwelcome.

Friday

I *had* to have company — I was
made for it, I think — so I made
friends with the animals. They are
just charming, and they have the
kindest disposition and the politest
ways; they never look sour, they
never let you feel that you are intruding, they smile at you and wag
their tail, if they've got one, and they
are always ready for a romp or an
excursion or anything you want to
propose. I think they are perfect
gentlemen. All these days we have
had such good times, and it hasn't
been lonesome for me, ever. Lonesome! No, I should say not. Why,
there's always a swarm of them
around—sometimes as much as four
or five acres—you can't count them;
and when you stand on a rock in the

Friday

midst and look out over the furry
expanse, it is so mottled and splashed
and gay with color and frisking sheen
and sun-flash, and so rippled with
stripes, that you might think it was
a lake, only you know it isn't; and
there's storms of sociable birds, and
hurricanes of whirring wings; and
when the sun strikes all that feathery
commotion, you have a blazing up of
all the colors you can think of, enough
to put your eyes out.

We have made long excursions,
and I have seen a great deal of the
world—almost all of it, I think; and
so I am the first traveller, and the
only one. When we are on the
march, it is an imposing sight—there's
nothing like it anywhere. For com-
fort I ride a tiger or a leopard, be-

Friday

cause it is soft and has a round back
that fits me, and because they are
such pretty animals; but for long distance or for scenery I ride the elephant. He hoists me up with his
trunk, but I can get off myself; when
we are ready to camp, he sits and I
slide down the back way.

The birds and animals are all
friendly to each other, and there are
no disputes about anything. They all
talk, and they all talk to me, but it
must be a foreign language, for I cannot make out a word they say; yet
they often understand me when I talk
back, particularly the dog and the
elephant. It makes me ashamed.
It shows that they are brighter than
I am, and are therefore my superiors.
It annoys me, for I want to be the

89

Friday

principal Experiment myself—and I intend to be, too.

I have learned a number of things, and am educated, now, but I wasn't at first. I was ignorant at first. At first it used to vex me because, with all my watching, I was never smart enough to be around when the water was running up-hill; but now I do not mind it. I have experimented and experimented until now I know it never does run up-hill, except in the dark. I know it does in the dark, because the pool never goes dry; which it would, of course, if the water didn't come back in the night. It is best to prove things by actual experiment; then you *know*; whereas if you depend on guessing and supposing and conjecturing, you will never get educated.

Friday

Some things you *can't* find out; but you will never know you can't by guessing and supposing: no, you have to be patient and go on experimenting until you find out that you can't find out. And it is delightful to have it that way, it makes the world so interesting. If there wasn't anything to find out, it would be dull. Even trying to find out and not finding out is just as interesting as trying to find out and finding out, and I don't know but more so. The secret of the water was a treasure until I *got* it; then the excitement all went away, and I recognized a sense of loss.

By experiment I know that wood swims, and dry leaves, and feathers, and plenty of other things; therefore by all that cumulative evidence you

91

Friday

When you cast up a feather it sails away on the air and goes out of sight; then you throw up a clod and it doesn't. It comes down, every time. I have tried it and tried it, and it is always so. I wonder why it is? Of course it *doesn't* come down, but why should it *seem* to? I suppose it is an optical illusion. I mean, one of them is. I don't know which one. It may be the feather, it may be the clod; I can't prove which it is, I can only demonstrate that one or the other is a fake, and let a person take his choice.

By watching, I know that the stars are not going to last. I have seen some of the best ones melt and run down the sky. Since one can melt, they can all melt; since they can all

Friday

melt, they can all melt the same
night. That sorrow will come — I
know it. I mean to sit up every
night and look at them as long as I
can keep awake; and I will impress
those sparkling fields on my memory,
so that by-and-by when they are
taken away I can by my fancy restore
those lovely myriads to the black sky
and make them sparkle again, and
double them by the blur of my tears.

After the Fall

When I look back, the Garden is a dream to me. It was beautiful, surpassingly beautiful, enchantingly beautiful; and now it is lost, and I shall not see it any more.

The Garden is lost, but I have found *him*, and am content. He loves me as well as he can; I love him with all the strength of my passionate nature, and this, I think, is proper to my youth and sex. If I ask myself why I love him, I find I do not know, and do not really much care to know; so I suppose that this kind of love is not a product of reasoning and statistics, like one's love for other reptiles and animals. I think that this must be so. I love certain birds because of their song; but I do not love Adam on account of his singing—no, it is not that;

94

After the Fall

the more he sings the more I do not
get reconciled to it. Yet I ask him to
sing, because I wish to learn to like
everything he is interested in. I am
sure I can learn, because at first I
could not stand it, but now I can. It
sours the milk, but it doesn't matter;
I can get used to that kind of milk.

It is not on account of his brightness that I love him—no, it is not that.
He is not to blame for his brightness,
such as it is, for he did not make it
himself; he is as God made him, and
that is sufficient. There was a wise
purpose in it; *that* I know. In time
it will develop, though I think it will
not be sudden; and, besides, there is
no hurry; he is well enough just as
he is.

It is not on account of his gracious

After the Fall

and considerate ways and his delicacy that I love him. No, he has lacks in these regards, but he is well enough just so, and is improving.

It is not on account of his industry that I love him—no, it is not that. I think he has it in him, and I do not know why he conceals it from me. It is my only pain. Otherwise he is frank and open with me, now. I am sure he keeps nothing from me but this. It grieves me that he should have a secret from me, and sometimes it spoils my sleep, thinking of it, but I will put it out of my mind; it shall not trouble my happiness, which is otherwise full to overflowing.

It is not on account of his education that I love him—no, it is not that. He is self-educated, and does really

After the Fall

know a multitude of things, but they
are not so.

It is not on account of his chivalry
that I love him—no, it is not that.
He told on me, but I do not blame
him; it is a peculiarity of sex, I think,
and he did not make his sex. Of
course I would not have told on him,
I would have perished first; but that
is a peculiarity of sex, too, and I do
not take credit for it, for I did not
make my sex.

Then why is it that I love him?
Merely because he is masculine, I think.

At bottom he is good, and I love
him for that, but I could love him
without it. If he should beat me
and abuse me, I should go on loving
him. I know it. It is a matter of
sex, I think.

97

After the Fall

He is strong and handsome, and I love him for that, and I admire him and am proud of him, but I could love him without those qualities. If he were plain, I should love him; if he were a wreck, I should love him; and I would work for him, and slave over him, and pray for him, and watch by his bedside until I died.

Yes, I think I love him merely because he is *mine* and is *masculine*. There is no other reason, I suppose. And so I think it is as I first said: that this kind of love is not a product of reasonings and statistics. It just *comes*—none knows whence—and cannot explain itself. And doesn't need to.

It is what I think. But I am only a girl, and the first that has examined

After the Fall

this matter, and it may turn out that in my ignorance and inexperience I have not got it right.

Forty Years Later

It is my prayer, it is my longing, that we may pass from this life together—a longing which shall never perish from the earth, but shall have place in the heart of every wife that loves, until the end of time; and it shall be called by my name.

But if one of us must go first, it is my prayer that it shall be I; for he is strong, I am weak, I am not so necessary to him as he is to me—life without him would not be life; how could I endure it? This prayer is also immortal, and will not cease from being offered up while my race continues. I am the first wife; and in the last wife I shall be repeated.

At Eve's Grave

ADAM: Wheresoever she was, *there* was Eden.

THE END

CPSIA information can be obtained at www.ICGtesting.com
Printed in the USA
LVOW13s0705090414

380974LV00001B/4/A